WILLIAM & KATE

CELEBRATING A ROYAL ROMANCE

ROBIN NUNN

First published in the
United Kingdom in 2010 by
Pavilion
10 Southcombe Street
London, W14 0RA

An imprint of Anova Books Company Limited

Design and layout © Hayden Media Limited, 2010
Photography © Nunn Syndication Limited

Produced by Hayden Media Limited, Middlesex, UK
Designed by Marcus Nichols

ISBN 9781862058439

A CIP catalogue record for this book is available from the British
Library.

Reproduction by Rival Colour Ltd, UK
Printed and bound by Butler Tanner & Dennis Ltd, Frome, UK

www.royalphoto.co.uk
www.anovabooks.com

For
FLORENCE GEORGINA ISABEL

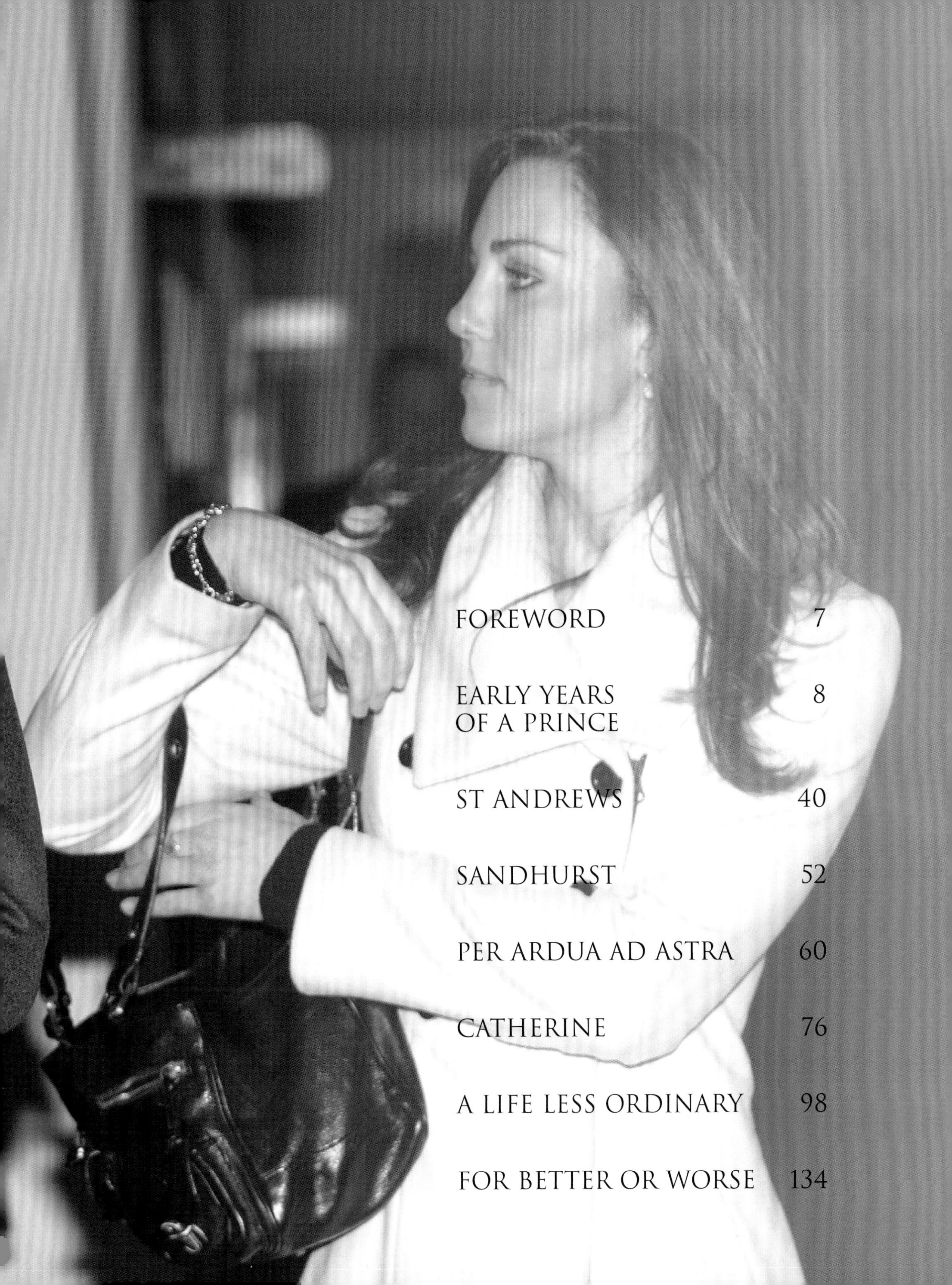

FOREWORD

This book was originally conceived and shaped on scraps of discarded notepaper in a bierkeller in Vilnius, Lithuania.

The date was 16 October 2006, and I was on the phone to my friend and colleague, Jonathan Hayden, discussing an idea that had been bouncing around in my head for some months: a new and up-to-date picture book telling the story of Prince William's journey from the steps of the Lindo wing at St Mary's Hospital, Paddington, London, into royal manhood, serving queen and country in the armed forces and his destiny as that of future king.

However, when we started researching the project on the future King William V, first-born son of Charles and Diana, Prince and Princess of Wales, it soon became apparent that it would be impossible to accurately chronicle his recent life without the inclusion of his long-term girlfriend, Miss Kate Middleton.

The media appeared to have already decided that the Prince had made his choice: a young woman from Berkshire named Catherine Elizabeth Middleton, Kate for short. Clearly credibility demanded that she would have to be included in the book.

I guess only time will tell, but this certainly posed us a challenging task because although I've spent the past 25 years or so having the professional privilege of photographing members of our royal family all over the world, I had hardly ever photographed Miss Middleton and, quite frankly, would have struggled to recognise her in a crowd or even if I sat next to her on the underground in London.

However, as time moved on and as fate would have it, Miss Middleton started appearing in the most unexpected of places, and it soon became apparent that at key moments in Prince William's evolving public life she was there, if not by his side then in very close proximity and always under the watchful eye of other senior members of the royal family – the Firm as it is often referred to.

We also examine how the other European monarchies are evolving into the 21st century with a series of fairytale weddings of their own Crown Princes and Crown Princesses and the huge affection subsequently shown to them by their modern day subjects.

So, in this my latest book, and with newspaper speculation starting to hit fever pitch we not only trace the life of William Arthur Philip Louis Windsor, the young man who will be king, we also attempt to illustrate his friendship with a young woman from an ordinary background who will one day, if ever she marries her prince, become our queen – Queen Catherine.

I hope you like the pictures.

Robin Nunn, Semonkong Lodge, Lesotho 16 June 2010.

"Nobody who has not been in the interior of a family, can say what the difficulties of any individual of that family may be."

Jane Austen, *Emma,* **1775–1817**

EARLY YEARS
OF A PRINCE

EARLY YEARS OF A PRINCE

At precisely 9.03pm on the 21 June, 1982, a 7lbs 10oz bouncing baby boy launched into his first few wails. William Arthur Philip Louis, first child to the Prince and Princess of Wales, had, thanks to his mother's influence already managed to break with a very private royal tradition: William was the first future heir to the throne to be born outside the walls of Buckingham Palace since the birth of Prince Edward (the future Edward VII) in 1841.

Diana's decision had not met with universal approval from within the royal household despite the young modern mother-to-be's understandable desire to give birth with the very best in neo-natal technology to hand. And, much to the surprise of other royal mothers, Diana also made it clear that she intended to breastfeed her child. She would have Charles's blessing on both counts, but from the outset raising their son in a manner appropriate for a future king would always be of paramount importance to both of them in distinctly different ways.

By the time of the announcement of Diana's pregnancy in November 1981, it was apparent to those close to the couple that all was not well. The private relationship between the newlyweds was a very different affair to the public show of affection that had been on offer to Fleet Street; nevertheless Charles's interest in his wife's pregnancy and welfare was unquestionably sincere.

Contrary to many reports, he was very much looking forward to becoming a father. Charles's own childhood had been governed by largely strict routine and, compared with more modern standards, a somewhat restricted and overly formal contact with his parents. By his own admission, his closest bond of trust and affection – which would later in life develop into the most supportive and intimate of his family relationships – was with his grandmother, Queen Elizabeth the Queen Mother. Reared mainly by his nanny, Mabel Anderson, Charles would spend months separated from his parents in the early years as they embarked on their relentless timetable of royal engagements, while his teenage years were spent in the austere surrounds of Gordonstoun, a boarding school in northeast Scotland.

Charles made it abundantly clear that his future child would be born into a closer, more intimate family situation and, once the pregnancy was confirmed, he became absolutely determined to mould himself into a model father. He would read a library of books on childbirth, labour and the role of modern fatherhood.

By now there existed an unquestioned love affair between the young Princess and the British people that had begun on the wedding day and showed no sign of cooling off. Wherever she went – officially or unofficially, publicly or privately – she would always be accompanied by dozens, sometime hundreds, of photographers and reporters, all desperate to record the minutiae of her life to satisfy the insatiable demand of the public's fascination with this new royal superstar. Without warning, and with little or no preparation, Diana had been elevated to the rank of a worldwide celebrity; a position she would inhabit for the rest of her tragically short life and a state of affairs she would view with considerable ambivalence.

A crude cardboard placard hung from the gates of St Mary's Hospital in Paddington proclaimed: 'It's a boy'. Two hours later Charles emerged onto the steps of the hospital to the sounds of 'For he's a jolly good fellow' as he greeted the hundreds of well-wishers and the ranks of assembled press. Commenting on Diana's protracted period of labour, he said, "Nearly 17 hours is a long time to wait. Obviously I'm relieved and delighted – I think it's marvellous. It's rather a grown up thing I've found. It's rather a shock."

Within 24 hours of the birth, the proud parents left hospital for home and William, wrapped up warmly in a pristine white lace shawl, was introduced briefly to the press with just his baby button nose and eyes visible. The couple were whisked back to Kensington Palace in a waiting car to begin life as parents and to face the realities of their family and public lives.

Publicly, little was seen of William in his first year – his most high profile 'engagement' being his christening by Dr Runcie, the Archbishop of Canterbury, on 4 August 1982 in the Music Room at Buckingham Palace. Surrounded by immediate family members, the service took place in the same room and he wore the same Honiton lace gown his father and every English monarch had worn since Edward VII.

At Christmas the same year William posed with his parents for photographers. For once Diana kept a low profile, holding William's favourite teething ring while father and son took centre stage playing together blissfully. For the first time the world had a glimpse of Charles as the doting father. His hands-on approach was proof that he was making a concerted effort to bond with his son. Charles had restricted his own official engagements in that crucial first year, and apart from a nine-day break with his wife in the Bahamas, made himself available to assist whenever and wherever possible.

In March 1983 the Prince and Princess of Wales undertook their first official tour together, flying to Australia and New Zealand. It was to be an arduous six-week trip and the couple's decision to take their young son with them prompted considerable public debate. At one point it was reported, quite wrongly as it turned out, that Diana was defying her mother-in-law's wishes by taking William on the trip, but there were genuine concerns that the 27-hour flight and numerous internal trips would take their toll on the nine-month-old Prince. The Foreign Office had argued on more than one occasion that: "It is not possible for the baby to accompany the royal couple." Not for the first or last time Diana stood her ground and made it clear that she could not and would not be parted from her son. After further consideration and a request by the Australian Prime Minister, Malcolm Fraser, it was finally decided that William would make the trip. In doing so he became the first royal baby to embark on an overseas trip – another break with tradition.

In June 1984 the royal family gathered together for the annual Trooping the Colour, the official ceremony that takes place in June each year at Horseguard's Parade in London to mark the Queen's birthday. After the formal ceremony, the royal family gathered on the balcony of Buckingham Palace to watch the RAF flypast and the first signs of strain between Diana and Charles began to creep into the public consciousness. Diana, now heavily pregnant with her second child, look decidedly glum, while Charles, absorbed by the pomp and the excitement of the day, appeared to disregard his wife's obvious distress.

William's second birthday seemed to bring the now warring Waleses closer together; likewise the arrival of Prince Henry, or Harry as he became known. At 4.20pm on 15 September 1984, the Princess gave birth to a 6lb 14oz boy. Although born in the same Lindo Wing of St Mary's Hospital in Paddington as his brother, the post-birth celebrations in the streets outside were muted in comparison to those that had greeted William's arrival two years earlier.

As second in line to the throne it was inevitable that William would take the lion's share of attention. The blond hair and blue eyes, so reminiscent of his mother, would always guarantee the perfect public image of a royal prince. It would be easy for the media and the general public to consign Harry to the role of the 'spare'. William, however, had inherited another of his mother's attributes and even at such a tender age, his compassion shone out. Immensely protective of Harry, his affection was evident from the first day and the jealousy that so often accompanies the birth of a younger sibling simply failed to materialise. Diana can take a great deal of credit for helping to establish a loving relationship between the brothers. She insisted that her eldest son should participate whenever possible in helping to feed, bath and change the baby. The boys played together for hours on end in the nursery at Kensington Palace and, even though William failed to at first grasp the process of sharing – particularly when it came to his favourite toy cars – a close bond developed between the pair: a bond that has grown stronger over the years and shows no sign of abating in adulthood.

William's first day at nursery school unsurprisingly became a huge media circus with photographers, reporters and television crews camped outside Mrs Jane Mynor's Nursery School in Notting Hill Gate, London.

At precisely 9.40am clutching a bright red Postman Pat flask full of orange juice William entered through the door marked Cygnets – later he would become a 'Little Swan' and, finally, a 'Big Swan', but for now it was the young Prince who was spreading his wings. Diana looked through a glass door with pride as William settled down to play with his new schoolmates. It was Diana's firm intention to give her children an upbringing that was as normal as possible, and here was three-year-old William integrating with society and, more importantly, mixing with children of his own age.

Even so, a future king educated outside the walls of Buckingham Palace requires unprecedented levels of security and protection. The windows of the nursery were replaced with bulletproof glass and a panic button was installed next to Mrs Mynor's desk. William's detective accompanied him at every session and it was widely reported at the time that an armed guard was always in close proximity.

Around this time an aspect of William's behaviour was beginning to seriously worry his parents. Tantrums were becoming all too commonplace; at nursery he was heard to say on more than one occasion, "If you don't do what I say then I'll have you arrested." Diatribes directed at staff at Kensington Palace left his parents red-faced. Things came to a head at the wedding of his uncle, Prince Andrew, to Sarah Ferguson. While the other pageboys and bridesmaids demonstrated exemplary behaviour, William fidgeted throughout the ceremony and, in front of millions watching on television, constantly poked out his tongue at whoever looked in his direction.

For Charles this was the straw that broke the camel's back and all his initial reservations regarding the appointment of William's nanny, Nanny Barnes, and her too liberal approach to the job seemed to be entirely justified. With William's imminent departure to Wetherby School it was decided that Barnes should leave Kensington Palace, a decision Diana went along with willingly as she had become increasingly concerned – jealous even – of the bond that had developed between Barnes and William.

However, it would be wrong to single out Barnes as being totally to blame for William's rebellious nature. With his parents' unavoidable and often extended absences, William simply failed to associate them with discipline: he saw only two people who showered him with love as compensation for their prolonged absences and endlessly busy lives. And William was old enough now to detect the obvious tensions that had developed between his parents.

By the time William was four his parents' marriage had deteriorated to the point where they were effectively leading separate lives. The couple looked increasingly strained during public appearances together and an uneasy front was put on for the watching media. Behind the scenes the battle lines had already been drawn. Charles had moved most of his belongings to Highgrove, his Gloucestershire residency, while Diana remained at Kensington Palace with the boys. The family would spend weekends together at the country retreat and although an illusion of happy families was played out, the weekends were far removed from the fun-loving, outgoing lifestyle that was encouraged by Diana. Nevertheless, William would grow to love the countryside and country pursuits.

On 10 September 1990, accompanied by both parents, looking dignified and the epitome of a young royal, William shook hands with Gerald Barber, the joint headmaster of Ludgrove – the Eton 'feeder' school in leafy Berkshire. He would struggle to adapt to his new surroundings. Phone calls to parents were barred, except in an emergency, and he would only return home every four weeks and during school holidays. William was often seen in tears in the first few weeks and Diana was a frequent visitor during his first term. As time progressed, however, William began to evolve from a somewhat tearful boy to a delightfully mannered young man, although he was still regarded as a somewhat aloof figure, behaviour almost certainly linked to the very public problems engulfing his parents' marriage.

Notwithstanding the efforts of Mr Barber to shield the young Prince from the excesses of the media, adolescent boys can be cruel and gossip-mongering took hold. It is a testament to William's strong character that he never allowed his personal worries to affect his education.

Indeed, William blossomed into a model academic student, finishing regularly in the top third of his class. His sporting talent also began to shine as he became the school's star basketball player while continuing his passion for swimming and football.

In November the Queen proclaimed 1992 her annus horribilis following the break-up not only of Charles's marriage but also that of the Duke and Duchess of York (Prince Andrew and Sarah Ferguson), and the disastrous fire at her beloved Windsor Castle. The following month on 9 December Prime Minister John Major announced to the House of Commons the separation of the Prince and Princess of Wales. "This decision has been reached amicably and they will continue to participate fully in the upbringing of their children. The Queen and the Duke of Edinburgh, though saddened, understand and sympathise with the difficulties that have led to this decision. Her Majesty and His Royal Highness particularly hope the intrusion into the privacy of the Prince and Princess may now cease." A forlorn and tragically optimistic hope when viewed in hindsight.

Although too young to be fully cognisant of all the facts, William believed Diana to be the innocent victim in the break-up of the marriage. His growing antipathy towards the press was further fuelled by the intense scrutiny under which both his mother and father now found themselves. It was rare to pick up a newspaper, especially the tabloid press, without a sensationalised story involving either parent and William would later confess that whenever he saw a picture of his parents in print his heart would sink and a sick feeling would develop in the pit of his stomach.

William was always closely associated with his mother, not least because of his striking physical resemblance to her that was becoming more apparent in his early teens.

Yet he also enjoyed the time he spent with other members of the royal family and, as future heir to the throne, he began to realise that the pomp and ceremony that he so disliked played a huge role in their everyday life and had to be learned and respected.

The first Christmas following the separation of his parents was spent at Sandringham with Charles and Harry, while Diana joined her brother at Althorp. In his early years William had found the presence of his grandmother somewhat daunting, but as he matured he began to warm to her and the Duke of Edinburgh, to understand the role of the royal family in society – and, indeed, his own position as future heir to the throne. He made a point of having tea with the Queen each week at Buckingham Palace, while the Duke instructed him in the finer points of shooting. At church that Christmas, William escorted the Queen Mother into the chapel of St Mary Magdalene and, in accordance with royal etiquette, he would now bow in his grandmother's presence.

In the weeks and months that followed the separation his achievements, both in and outside the classroom, had tailed off dramatically. But supported by the love and affection being provided by both his parents, and by virtue of his hard work, the young Prince passed his Common Entrance Exam for Eton. He was also helped in no small part by a ruling that barred the press from intruding on his studies.

After becoming a teenager in July 1995, William made a quantum leap just three months later when his life began at Eton, the most famous and celebrated public school of them all. Situated by the River Thames near Windsor, Eton College was founded by Henry VI and has been responsible for the education of the sons of Europe's most well-heeled and powerful families. Immersed in tradition, Eton has produced one Northern Ireland and nineteen British prime ministers. Despite its history and traditions, Eton is a forward-looking establishment, which prides itself on the academic achievements of its pupils, many of whom come from varying social and ethnic backgrounds. Indeed, it was this positive and ecumenical attitude that most impressed Charles when he visited the school before William's arrival. Looking back at his own school days at Gordonstoun, Charles recalled that for him it was not unusual to have to endure an ice cold shower on a winter's morning before being forced to play rugby on snow-laden pitches in the skimpiest of clothes. He regarded his time at Gordonstoun as 'a prison sentence' and had no wish to see his children suffer the same misery and discomfort. Diana had an additional reason to be happy: her brother and father were Old Etonians and the college was just a 30-minute journey from Kensington Palace.

William's progress at Eton was emphatic to the considerable delight of his parents and also his grandmother. With Windsor Castle's close proximity, William would be a Sunday afternoon visitor whenever the Queen was in residency and it was during these intimate meetings that she would help prepare her grandson for his future role. They would often meet at 4.00pm in the Oak Drawing Room for tea. These occasions would provide William with an opportunity to discover the workings of a modern monarchy and see for himself the famous 'boxes' – the red boxes containing details of the Queen's forthcoming engagements and the blue boxes holding documents from the Home Office.

Back at Eton, William's enthusiasm and never-say-die attitude on the sports field won him the respect of team-mates. As captain of the school swimming team – he was Eton's fastest swimmer for ten years – and with his desire to try out canoeing, water polo and judo, William was regarded as a popular true all-rounder. His life had found a purpose and rhythm despite the continuing antagonism between his parents.

In the aftermath of the separation Charles co-operated with renowned broadcaster Jonathan Dimbleby who was writing a substantial biography of the Prince. In what was to prove a watershed moment, which would define for many years to come how Prince Charles would be viewed by the public, he gave Dimbleby a warts-and-all tele-vision interview, shown on the BBC in June 1994. Shock and outrage reverberated around the world as Charles admitted to committing adultery with Camilla Parker Bowles throughout his marriage to Diana.

Diana sought her revenge in an interview for BBC's *Panorama* programme broadcast the following November.

In a candid, 55-minute interview with correspondent Martin Bashir, the Princess discussed her husband's affair, her subsequent depression and eating disorders, and her belief that there was a Palace conspiracy orchestrated against her. Perhaps the most damning was the admission that she too had been unfaithful with former Life Guards' officer, James Hewitt.

What William would have made of this would be pure conjecture, but it should be remembered that he had, up to this point, never met Camilla Parker Bowles.

While Diana was upset at the impact of the revelations on both her sons, the interview somehow transformed her life. To a degree, it set her free from the shackles of her failed royal marriage and she would be seen by many as a beautiful, liberated woman in her own right.

On 28 August 1996 divorce proceedings were finalised and although she lost her HRH status, she would be known henceforth as Diana, Princess of Wales. Under even greater public scrutiny she decided to cut back on her official engagements. The number of charities she actively supported was reduced to just six.

Her divorce and subsequent retirement from many aspects of public life left the Princess with more time and liberty, and a fatal underestimation of the obsessive fascination that the press and public would continue to have in her life. Concern was also growing in the royal household that Diana's behaviour was becoming increasingly wilful.

Shortly after Diana and her boys' holiday at Harrods owner Mohamed Al Fayed's villa in St Tropez in July 1997, a British newspaper announced, in what they claimed was a world exclusive, that Diana had found a new love, naming Al Fayed's son Dodi. She and Dodi were photographed in late July on Fayed's yacht as they sailed along the Cote d'Azur.

Diana's last public appearance was in Bosnia in mid-August where she was involved in her anti-landmine work.

It was proving a difficult summer for William; there was little doubt that he was torn, trying to remain loyal to both parents and splitting his time between them. He had enjoyed the glamorous lifestyle holidaying with his mother in St Tropez, but he also loved the outdoor life – hunting, shooting, fishing and riding – that made up his time at Balmoral, where he stayed throughout August with Harry, his father and the Queen and the Duke of Edinburgh.

While the royal household slept on the night of Saturday, 30 August 1997, Charles was woken at 1.00am with the news that Diana had been severely injured in a car accident. He had been made aware by the Queen's deputy private secretary, Sir Robin Janvrin, that while there had been fatalities and although Diana's injuries were serious, her condition was not thought to be life-threatening. There was no reason at this stage to upset the princes unnecessarily so they were left to sleep. Charles remained in his study to await further news. Two hours later all hopes that had been raised within Balmoral were extinguished and in its place came total devastation: Diana had died on the operating table of the Pitié-Salpêtrière hospital in Paris.

Little is still known of the painful hours that followed. It is believed that Charles let the boys sleep until early morning before breaking the news to them, after which they spent much of the morning with their grandparents.

But even the sudden devastating loss of their mother did not prevent strict adherence to royal duty. Just hours after receiving the news, the young princes, clearly upset and in shock, attended Sunday service at the nearby Crathie Kirk. It was a tradition that whenever the royal family were in residence at Balmoral, they would attend the Sunday service, and on the 31 August 1997, things would be no different.

Following an autopsy in a private mortuary in Fulham, Diana's body was transferred to the Chapel Royal, St James's Palace, where crowds flocked in their hundreds of thousands to lay flowers and sign books of condolence. As the mounting national grief gathered pace, parts of London almost came to a standstill: Buckingham Palace, The Mall and Kensington Palace became vast seas of floral tributes.

There is little doubt that the royal family underestimated the deep affection many people felt for Diana; regardless of her divorce from Charles and arguably from the rest of the royal family, Diana had been, as Tony Blair so aptly put it, the 'People's Princess' and was, after all, the mother of the future king.

On 5 September Princes William and Harry accompanied their father on a walkabout at Kensington Palace, where their evident courage reduced many onlookers to tears. It was then on to St James's Palace where Diana and her boys would be reunited for the very last time. As they approached the Palace and observed more floral tributes – some five feet deep in places – the boys were visibly distressed and almost overwhelmed by the events of the week, yet they managed to hold their emotions in check, William would glance up in that way so reminiscent of his mother and smile shyly before offering a hand and a polite: "Thank you for coming."

This day had proved something: William, for so long the focus of so much attention, had in the past only appeared in pubic to appease the insatiable demands of the press. But this situation was unique; this was not and could not be stage-managed, and those who walked away from St James's Palace that night were left in no doubt that among the achievements in her short life, Diana's greatest legacy would be this young boy who had the character, warmth and innate compassion he would need for his role as future king in the 21st century.

3 January, 1988: The old estate fire engine at Sandringham exerts a powerful attraction for a little prince.

(Previous page) **22 June, 1982:** The proud parents leave St Mary's hospital, Paddington, with Prince William. "Give us another one, Charlie!" shouted an onlooker. The Prince shook his head and replied, "You will have to ask my wife about that." Before adding, "Bloody hell, give us a chance!"

12 June, 1990: Tug-of-war at Wetherby School sports day.

16 August, 1985: The royal family disembarks from HMY *Britannia* at Aberdeen harbour after cruising the Western Isles.

19 April, 1992: Easter Sunday, Windsor.

1 March, 1991: Diana decides that William, at the age of eight, is ready for his first official engagement. As the future Prince of Wales it is considered appropriate that his inaugural trip should be to Cardiff on St David's Day.

23 March, 1989: Easter Sunday at Windsor and William is already perfecting his handshake in preparation for a life of royal duty.

28 January, 1995: It was always Diana's desire to give her children as normal an upbringing as possible. Having seen at first hand the results of Charles's restricted childhood, she was determined to give her boys the chance to experience everyday life. Whether it was a trip to Alton Towers, a visit to the West End to see the latest film or even a trip on London's Underground system, she planned excursions with her sons' future roles in mind. Diana was respectful of William's royal destiny, extremely proud that one day he would be king. A trip to the Chicago Rib Shack, at the time the boys' favourite restaurant, was a typical example of Diana's influence.

20 June, 1984: In an extraordinary moment of photographic coincidence, the Princess of Wales is snapped passing the then royal journalist Andrew Morton at the Guards Polo Club after Royal Ascot. Eight years later Morton's book *Diana: Her True Story* would send shock waves around the world, forever changing the relationship between the royal family and the nation.

3 December, 1993: We had heard on the Fleet Street grapevine that there was going to be a big announcement about the future of Diana, Princess of Wales. When it became known exactly what Diana was going to say, that she would retire from public life, a shaken media corps went very silent. [RN]

3 December, 1993: Diana announces her withdrawal from public life at a charity lunch. "I hope you can find it in your hearts to understand and give me the time and space that has been lacking in recent years". Many were shocked and saddened at the loss of such a charismatic figure from the world stage and interpreted her remarks as a tired and angst-ridden complaint at the intense and constant intrusion by sections of the media.

10 August, 1997: This is the last frame I ever took of Diana. She was in Bosnia on behalf of her anti-landmine work when we were invited to the press call at Balmoral. There is a special poignancy to this picture as Diana pushes away an intrusive cameraman. I never saw her alive again. [RN]

10 August, 1997: Diana comforts a war widow in Sarajevo. Her compassion is obvious.

31 August, 1997: Charles had been woken at 1:00am with the news that Diana had been severely injured in a car accident in Paris. Within two hours came the devastating news that Diana had died on the operating table. Nevertheless, adherence to royal duty remained paramount and the family would attend the regular Sunday service at the nearby Crathie Kirk that morning.

4 September, 1997: Five days after Diana's death, the public get their first glimpse of the young princes as they view tributes left at the gates of Balmoral Castle.

5 September, 1997: The royal family, including the Queen and the Queen Mother, board a plane at Aberdeen airport to fly back to England.

6 September, 1997: At 10.25am, William and Harry, heads bowed, along with their father, Prince Charles, their grandfather, Prince Philip and Diana's brother, Earl Spencer, wait on The Mall outside St James's Palace to accompany their mother on her final journey.

11 January, 2010: William had the best hugging teacher in his late mother. Here he is with pupil Darren Pearty at Eresby School in Spilsby, England.

1 October, 1995: Diana hugs Laurence Chambers at the National Institute of Conductive Education in Birmingham.

25 December, 2008: Sporting a beard grown while on a Special Boat Service exercise in November, the Prince is said to be the spitting image of his great great grandfather, George V. The new look won the approval of many of his fans gathered outside St Mary Magdalene church on the Queen's estate at Sandringham. Said one, "Today I called out to William, 'Where's my Christmas kiss?' He looked at me and said, 'Oh, go on then - but just one kiss'. He put his cheek next to mine and I kissed him right on his beard. It was lovely, so soft, not scratchy. He must have put conditioner on it. I can't stop shaking, I'm so excited."

"The main things which seem
to me important on their own
account, and not merely as
means to other things, are
knowledge, art, instinctive
happiness, and relations
of friendship or affection."
Bertrand Russell 1872–1970

ST ANDREWS

2

ST ANDREWS

Sometime in the year 2000, Kate Middleton, a Marlborough School-educated teenager of solid, commendably middleclass parentage, would have been quietly deliberating, like many thousands of others, where exactly she should pursue her continuing studies. An apt pupil, she could have a choice of the best universities in the land; as Kate reflected and made her eventual decision in favour of St Andrews University in the northeast corner of Scotland, she can surely have had no presentiment of the extraordinary life-changing consequences the decision would bring.

Enrolling in a degree course to read the History of Art would launch her into the orbit of another student, William Arthur Philip Louis Windsor – second in line to the British throne and Britain's future king. In due course they would share a house together on the edge of the Scottish town and embark on a romance that to this day remains a source of intense media interest and speculation around the globe.

An institution of considerable renown, St Andrews was founded in 1413, is the oldest university in Scotland and the third oldest in the United Kingdom. It was quickly recognised as one of the leading universities of Europe and by the late middle ages had three endowed colleges: St Salvator's founded in 1450; St Leonard's (now united with St Salvator's) founded in 1511 and St Mary's founded in 1537. Steeped in history, it dominates the small town where it overlooks a wind-swept sandy beach and, of course, the world-famous golf courses of the same name.

Earlier in the year, Prince William had explained his choice of university stating that he didn't want to go to an English university, "because I have lived there and wanted to get away and try something else". He also pointed out that he would be seeing a lot of Wales in the future, but he loved the hills, the mountains and, indeed, the spirit of the Scottish people themselves. Sentiments that would have

pleased members of the royal household who have strong and enduring ties with Scotland.

William would not be the first heir to the throne to attend university. Edward VII had been to three universities; Edward VIII had been to Oxford and, when there was no expectation that he would later be king, the Prince's grandfather, George VI, had attended Cambridge, as would William's father.

In fact Charles's arrival at Cambridge and the behind-the-scenes deliberations, involving the Prime Minister of the day among several other establishment figures, that had gone into deciding on the choice of university and college were in stark contrast to the apparent informality of William's arrival at St Andrews on the 24 September 2001.

In December 1965 a meeting had taken place at Buckingham Palace at the invitation of the Queen. Those invited included the then Prime Minister Harold Wilson; the Archbishop of Canterbury, Michael Ramsey; the chief of the Defence Staff, Lord Mountbatten; the Dean of Windsor, Robin Woods; and Sir Charles Wilson, Principal and Vice-Chancellor of Glasgow University. The Queen asked her distinguished guests to form a committee under the chairmanship of the Duke of Edinburgh to discuss the further education of the Prince of Wales. That the Prince would have to enter one or more of the armed services was unquestioned; the issue for the *ad hoc* committee was whether he would also go to university.

Notwithstanding Harold Wilson's formidable lobbying for Oxford – where he had been such a distinguished student – and Mountbatten's forceful urging that the Prince should be sent straight to the Royal Navy College, Dartmouth, it had been decided, after several months, that Trinity College, Cambridge, would welcome the Prince at the start of the autumn term in 1967. In an attempt to play down the visibility of his arrival at Trinity, Charles bowled up to the college on the first day of term at the wheel of a Mini, from which his first glimpse of academia was "the serried ranks of various trousered legs, from which I had to distinguish the Master and Senior Tutor."

Thirty-four years later an altogether different car carefully negotiated the narrow, cobbled entrance to St Salvator's College. A crowd of several thousand had gathered in a mood of welcoming curiosity to watch as the 19-year-old Prince William emerged in the uniform of a typical modern-day student of jeans, trainers and sweater to shake the hand of the university principal, Dr Brian Lang, and to be greeted by a clutch of other academic dignitaries. William, looking somewhat taken aback by the size of the welcoming committee, entered the college and – with the acquiesce of the British media who had in consultation with Clarence House agreed that they, in return for a handful of pre-arranged photo-opportunities, would stay away from the Prince for the four years of his degree course – strolled casually out of the public eye.

Prince William's earlier reference to Wales was an interesting aside; unintentionally, it again prompted comparisons: that William's four years at St Andrews might develop in relative normality when set against the insistence on a programme of regular royal duties and necessary accommodations to the politics of the day that had characterised Prince Charles's experience during his three years at Cambridge. After a mere four terms at Trinity, Prince Charles's new life at Cambridge had been interrupted by an uncomfortable but ultimately successful term at the University College of Wales at Aberystwyth – something that had come about at the request of the then Secretary of State for Wales, George Thomas (later Speaker of the House of Commons) two years earlier. Although thought to be an appropriate lead up to the formal investiture of the Prince of Wales, which had been arranged for 1 July 1969, it was undoubtedly a political, rather than an educational decision.

A surge of nationalism in Wales had found expression in a simplified demand that Welsh should become the official language of the principality, which in practice meant a stampede towards bureaucratic bi-lingualism, since only a modest percentage of the Welsh population could read, let alone speak, the language. Prince Charles would inevitably have to accommodate the mood of the day and, in an eight-week crash course, learn the rudiments of the language.

At the end of the term he would attend the Urdd National Eisteddfod, where he would make his first significant public speech. He had agreed, in response to a challenge from the organisers, to make it in Welsh. Ultimately, his delivery won him a standing ovation from the audience of 6,000, who, at the very least, admired his courage. The Prince remarked that he felt the whole experience had been 'interesting'.

Awarded a lower second class degree, not only was Charles the first heir to the throne to secure a degree, but also in his final year it was judged by the Master of Trinity that he had been academically handicapped by far too many royal engagements.

William craved a degree of normality and anonymity that would have mystified his father at a similar age – albeit a privileged normality far removed from the lives of most people – and he would try desperately to fit in, or at least not stand out, as he settled down to study History of Art, and Anthropology in his first year.

While Eton College has its own brand of austerity and engenders confidence, bordering on arrogance some might say, in its alumni, there is no doubt that William, used to the privileges accorded to a prince, of a life lived in palaces and grand country houses, found the initial transition difficult. Trust was at the heart of it; during his first term William's lifestyle was so circumscribed by discretion and his reluctance to let anyone close that the anticipated feeling of freedom and enjoyment of a relatively carefree student life failed to materialise.

Kate Middleton had settled well in to St Salvator's on the floor above William. Unlike many of the girls who seemed determined to catch the Prince's eye, she did not evince an air of desperation or a painful determination to woo William when in his company. In the first term she had become a member of the Prince's tentative circle of friends. There were areas of common ground – Kate had spent part of her gap year in Chile as had William; she loved sport including skiing as well as being an accomplished hockey and netball player. Living close to each other in the halls of residence meant it was both easy and perfectly natural that they would see each other regularly – in the same bars, across the tennis net and in the lecture room.

A crisis, however, was looming. By April 2002 stories began to circulate that the Prince was disenchanted with his course and life at St Andrews in general. Possibly bored and homesick, he was regularly making the nine hundred mile round trip to Highgrove at weekends. Both Prince Charles and the Duke of Edinburgh were supportive but unequivocal and urged William to "stick with it." William later said that chats with his father had been a great help, "We chatted a lot and in the end we both realised – I definitely realised – that I had to come back."

Kate had had her own moments of doubt, homesickness and frustrations with her course, and there is little doubt that she was now even more of a trusted confidante for William. Kate is widely credited with the suggestion that William change his course rather than give it up entirely. The prospect of the future heir to the throne dropping out in his first year of university was a matter of serious concern to the monarchy. Remembering how harsh had been the criticism levelled at both Prince Edward and the royal family in general when he had quit the Royal Marines officer training course after just four months,

Palace officials felt sure that William's departure from St Andrews would give licence to the media, and many republican-minded commentators, to tear into the royal family yet again.

A decision to switch the Prince's course from the History of Art to Geography – a subject the Prince had always felt an affinity for as it chimed with his desire "[to] do something with the environment" – was an entirely acceptable compromise. William immediately felt happier and soon began to integrate himself more thoroughly into university life, flourishing in the lecture room and demonstrating his sporting talents by gaining his colours with the university water polo team.

As evidence of his renewed enthusiasm he made his first public appearance at a student fashion show at the end of his first year. He turned up to cheer on Kate, who stunned the audience in a risqué black lace dress over a bandeau bra and black bikini bottoms. William took his seat, and in doing so, after a Sunday paper was tipped off by a fellow student, ensured that Kate and their friendship was brought to the attention of the British public.

Quite how unsettled William was in his first year is open to conjecture, but his decision to set up home with three friends, including Kate, in a house by the famous golf links in his second year would suggest he had overcome his early problems.

The deal or *entente cordiale* with press was holding up well, despite the reports on the fashion show and the initial speculation about Kate, but the fact that she and William were co-habiting and clearly entirely comfortable in each other's company meant there was growing public interest. So much so that in May 2003, Kate's father felt it necessary to deny reports that Kate was William's girl-friend. "I can categorically confirm they are no more than friends," he said. The media begged to differ and would now be watching her every move.

A little under a year later William and Kate's romance went well and truly public when the *Sun* newspaper published pictures of the couple on the slopes at the ski resort of Klosters in Switzerland. Palace officials had long feared that the unofficial pact with the British media to safeguard the privacy of Princes William and Harry would break down at the first sign of a girlfriend. Clarence House reacted furiously, taking punitive action against the *Sun*, which was vigorous in its own defence issuing a statement that argued that there was now a *bona fide* public interest in knowing what romantic interests might be developing in the Prince's life. One of William's girlfriends could become Queen one day it was pointed out, and her

subjects will be entitled to know all about her. It was, it has to be said, a fair point.

No attempt was made by William to deny that Kate was his girlfriend after the pictures appeared. Two years on from the fashion show and 'that dress', William had an official girlfriend.

A year later in March 2005 and observers in Klosters again – this time to cover Prince Charles's annual ski trip – were treated to overwhelming evidence of the deepening relationship between William and Kate and the degree to which she had been assimilated into the heart of his family. For the first time Charles was photographed with Kate as they chatted together, and the only possible interpretation was that William had, at some point, made the serious and difficult decision to introduce Kate into his other and inescapable royal life. To turn back now, to deny Kate was going to be a important and permanent fixture in his life would not just affect the happiness of the couple themselves, but would be the cause of world-wide comment and judgement.

Three months later on 23 June 2005 in Younger Hall both William and Kate graduated as Master of Arts. Catherine Middleton had already stepped up to the stage ahead of the Prince to receive her degree when, with his father and stepmother and royal grandparents watching on, William Wales was called the centre-stage pulpit. There he knelt before the Chancellor of St Andrews, Sir Kenneth Dover, and was tapped lightly on the head with a 17th-century scarlet cap, the academic hood was hooked over his shoulders, and with a 2:1 class degree – beating his father's 2:2 from Cambridge, making him one of the most academically successful royals – four years of study was over.

A sort of reality beckoned. William would fly to New Zealand to meet the touring British and Irish Lions (rugby) team and carry out his first solo engagements on behalf of the Queen – attending ceremonies in Wellington and Auckland to mark the anniversary of the end of World War II.

After that it would be a series of work experience placements, one of which would be at RAF Valley and with a nearby mountain rescue team. "Joining a mountain rescue team really appealed to me as I can learn at first hand how these amazing people help save lives on a regular basis." Prophetic words whose significance would only become apparent three years later.

As for Kate, well she would bide her time and make a new entrance on to the royal stage worthy of a leading lady.

4 June, 2005: When I first saw Kate I barely recognised her and it was only the media scrum which formed that gave away the fact she had arrived. A winning smile I have come to know. [RN]

4 June, 2005: Kate joins William at the society wedding of Hugh van Cutsem to Rose Astor.

23 June, 2005: Already established in the public's mind as Prince William's girlfriend, Catherine Middleton (as she will be called when summoned to the stage), receives her degree in the History of Art.

23 June, 2005: In front of his father and stepmother and his royal grandparents William kneels before Sir Kenneth Dover, Chancellor of St Andrews. Tapped lightly on the head with a 17th-century scarlet cap and with his red and black academic hood hooked over his shoulders, four years of study are over. William is now a Master of Arts and the real world beckons.

"Nowadays people's visual imagination is so much more sophisticated, so much more developed, particularly in young people, that now you can make an image which just slightly suggests something, they can make of it what they will."

Robert Doisneau 1912–1994

SANDHURST

SANDHURST

"If you look at the careers of successful officers, you will find that, no matter how clever they may have been, what really matters is how they related to people under their command. It is an art not a science, and it needs constant attention and refinement to achieve the highest standards. It was not by chance that the motto chosen for the Royal Military Academy is Serve to Lead."
From Her Majesty The Queen's speech made following the Sovereign's Parade at the Royal Military Academy Sandhurst, 12 April 2006.

Spoken without apparent irony, the carefully chosen words addressed to the 220 cadets from Commissioning Course 052 as they passed out after the 44-weeks training, contained much that might pass for the philosophy underpinning the successful workings of the monarchy itself. Admittedly, the long shadow cast by the bitter divorce and untimely death of the Princess of Wales has shrunk to folkloric memory, roused only to public consciousness by media-driven and now waning 'anniversaries' and obsessive conspiracists. But still, for the royal family, the right sort of good news involving one of their own is always to be welcomed, and today the most vigorously entertaining member of the Firm, an occasionally boisterous liability, stood centre-stage in boots polished to a shine of mirror-like perfection. Prince Harry was now a commissioned officer who would shortly join the Household Cavalry's Blues and Royals as a 2nd Lieutenant, giving the British Army a mighty and entirely predictable headache in the process.

Watching his younger brother, Prince William might have reflected on his own fateful words offered up in an interview before leaving St Andrews: "…the last thing I want to do is be mollycoddled or wrapped up in cotton wool, because if I was to join the Army I'd want to go where my men went and I'd want to do what they did. I would not want to be kept back for being precious, or whatever, that's the last thing I'd want. It's the most humiliating thing and it would be something I'd find very awkward to live with…".

Sincerely felt no doubt; the Sovereign is, of course, the Head of the Armed Forces, and she or he alone can declare war or peace. Britain's monarchy is intimately intertwined with the Services – the Queen's father, George VI, fought in the battle of Jutland in May 1916 as a 20-year-old Sub-Lieutenant in the Royal Navy and her son, Prince Andrew, flew as a second pilot in Sea King helicopters on anti-submarine and transport duties during the Falklands campaign in 1982. The Queen, for whom duty is paramount, would, in all likelihood accept the notion of her grandsons commanding their men in battle.

However, in a society clearly troubled by its military misadventures in Iraq and Afghanistan, the logistical and security complications of having the future heir to the throne or the 'spare' dropped into a war zone was, to most people's way of thinking, madness. Harry would eventually go to war, but have his tour of duty cut short once a foreign Internet site blew his anonymity. For Prince William, leading from the front was never going to be a realistic option.

Eight months later and the Queen allowed herself a smile; another Sovereign's Parade on a crisp December day and Her Majesty was enjoying herself. Inspecting the cadets, she had reached her grandson standing to attention and towering over her. William, like Harry, would go on to join the Blues and Royals, but Harry's deployment predicament would mean serious decisions would have to be made by the Army.

The youthful days of princes are full of firsts and lasts. Their lives must be lived more thoroughly than most; so much to be seen and done in preparation for a life of service. But some things once experienced need to be quietly put away and revisited only rarely: William graduated the day after an official police report, three years in the making, concluded that the car crash that had killed his mother was an accident. With his brother, the Prince asked for speculation about conspiracy theories surrounding her death to stop.

This December day had its other portents.

The order of precedence was settled by the House of Lords in 1539 and concerns itself with such matters as the order in which people march in procession (though here people usually move in reverse order of precedence, the least to the fore, the most important to the rear), are announced at gatherings or are listed in an official description of some ceremonial functions. In short, it is a rare thing for anyone to upstage Her Majesty The Queen. And that was presumably the last thing intended, but Kate Middleton's arrival as Prince William's guest in the company of Jamie Lowther-Pinkerton, private secretary to the Princes William and Harry was simply too newsworthy, too much of a statement.

And that coat, which had picture editors around the world scrabbling for pictures of Diana at her most glamorous, outshone even the uniformed splendour on show.

It was the entrance of a future star, possibly – if she could stay the course.

15 December, 2006: Kate is Prince William's guest at the Sovereign's Parade at the Sandhurst Military Academy. Significantly, she makes her entrance in the company of Jamie Lowther-Pinkerton, Private Secretary to Princes William and Harry. Kate's red coat reminds many observers of Diana at her most glamorous.

15 December, 2006: Many eyes were on Kate Middleton sitting among friends and relatives of the other cadets in the general stands.

15 December, 2006: As 2nd Lieutenant Wales marched with his fellow officer cadets, Kate leant forward smiling widely at him as he passed within a few feet. The Prince, forced to concentrate on the exacting manoeuvres, could not respond and maintained a strict military demeanour.

"It is the greatest shot of
adrenaline to be doing what
you have wanted to do so badly.
You almost feel like you could
fly without the plane."

Charles Lindbergh 1902–1974

PER ARDUA
AD ASTRA

PER ARDUA AD ASTRA

And what have kings that privates have not too,
Save ceremony, save general ceremony?
King Henry V Act IV Scene 1

Speaking publicly about Prince Harry's recall from active service in Helmand Province, Afghanistan, The Chief of the General Staff, General Sir Richard Dannatt was forthright: "We weighed up the factors and it was quite clear that the right thing to do, now that the story had become as widely public as it had, was to say 10 weeks has been a great contribution in our judgement. The risks of him staying now outweigh the benefits of him staying."

The Sovereign is Head of the Armed Forces and the historically intimate connection between the monarch and the three branches of the services meant that, post-university, Prince William could certainly expect to enter the forces, even if for a limited time. As future king, William would be pressed to 'do time' in the Army, RAF and Navy, and undergo a wide range of training and attachments in preparation for his future role.

No doubt the Navy, as the Senior Service, hoped the Prince would follow in the footsteps of his father, grandfather, great grandfather and great great grandfather, and enrol in the Royal Naval College, Dartmouth. Perhaps mindful of the consequences of the inevitable lengthy absences eventual shipboard duty would entail, William, who had been a member of the Eton cadet forces and spent time with the Welsh Guards on Salisbury Plain and in the jungles of Belize, decided instead to train at the Royal Military Academy Sandhurst and take a commission in the Blues and Royals – a cavalry regiment of the British Army, part of the Household Cavalry.

While the regiment was formed in 1969 from the merger of The Royal Horse Guards, which was known as 'The Blues', and The Royal Dragoons, which was known as 'The Royals', it is one of two regiments of the Household Division (a military unit that provides ceremonial and protective duties for the monarch) that can trace its lineage back to the New Model Army (formed in 1645 by the Parliamentarians in the English Civil War). The Colonel-in-Chief of the regiment is Her Majesty The Queen and the Colonel is HRH The Princess Royal.

No-one doubts for a moment that both Princes William and Harry's desire to serve Queen and Country on the frontline is entirely sincere. As trained and professional serving officers, to be kept out of harm's way – however justified the reasoning for such a decision – must rankle deeply. It is entirely to be expected that both would want to get their teeth into worthwhile and responsible jobs: to serve with and lead the men under their command. In years to come, Prince William, as part of his royal duties, must expect to make regular visits to Service establishments, to Royal Naval ships, and to meet servicemen and women of all ranks and their families, both in the United Kingdom and overseas. A duty that will be all the more enjoyable, acknowledged and welcomed when there exists a shared experience of active service.

Much of this nation's history can be seen through a lens that is the lives of its monarchs; at the heart of great events and with an innate conservatism that seems to slow time, the Queen and her immediate forebears bridge and define distinct ages – ages that seem on the one hand amazingly remote, and on the other to have unarguable resonance with many of today's dilemmas. The Queen's father (and Queen Victoria's great grandson), Prince Albert (later George VI), had attended Royal Naval College, Dartmouth in 1911 and was commissioned as a mid-shipman in September 1913; a year later he began service in World War I.

On the morning of 31 May 1916, over 250 British and German warships steamed on a convergent course to a rendezvous unanticipated by the Germans, off the Jutland coast of Denmark. A new and aggressive admiral, Reinhard Scheer, had taken charge of the German High Fleet in January that year and his decision to take the whole of his fleet into the North Sea, something never ventured before, was based on the mistaken belief that the British would have no advance knowledge of his movements. With Admirals Jellicoe and Beatty's ships advancing to an interception too far from port for Scheer to escape to safety during daylight hours, Britain's Grand Fleet had a great victory in prospect.

A 20-year-old Sub-Lieutenant aboard HMS *Collingwood*, known to his shipmates as Mr Johnson, would have viewed the imminent battle with all the excitement and trepidation of any young officer as yet untested in war. Prince Albert, as he was more correctly titled, would be the last British monarch to see action in battle – an inconclusive and still much debated battle that ultimately cost the lives of more than 6,000 British sailors (the Germans suffered far fewer losses of both men and ships) and for which both sides made strident claims of victory.

With monarchs, historical coincidences are plentiful: the Flagship of Admiral Jellicoe, the Commander in Chief Grand Fleet during the Battle of Jutland was HMS *The Iron Duke*. One of four capital ships built around 1911 at a cost of nearly £2 million, 92 years later Prince William would serve on board the Portsmouth-based frigate and third Royal Naval ship to bear the name, a ship that had been built in 1990 at a cost of £140 million.

Ill health prevented Prince Albert from seeing further action in the War. In 1918 the Naval Air Service's training establishment at Cranwell transferred to the control of the recently created Royal Air Force and Prince Albert, who had been appointed Officer in Charge of Boys, became the first royal to serve in the RAF. He would marry Lady Elisabeth Bowes-Lyon in 1923 in Westminster Abbey wearing the full dress uniform of a Group Captain.

For much of 2007 Prince William experienced regimental life and, after passing an intensive specialist troop leader's course, commanding a troop of four Scimitar armoured reconnaissance vehicles. In January 2008 he would begin an attachment with the Royal Air Force allowing him to realise a lifetime ambition to learn to fly.

William's father, who had initially learned to fly during his time at Cambridge University, had successfully converted to a Jet Provost at RAF Cranwell in 1971, going solo after eight hours in the air with instructor Squadron Leader Richard Johns (later Air Marshal), rather than the usual ten hours. Prince William would mirror his father's achievement by becoming the first member of his class to fly solo. Prince William it seems is a talented pilot. An assessment Wing Commander Andy Lovell, who helped train the Prince and was responsible for judging his performances prior to the Prince completing the course, endorsed: "William was very good. I was very impressed by his flying skills. He had a natural handling ability and he was very quick to learn. He responded well to instructions and demonstrated plenty of spare capacity. He was a very good student all round."

On 11 April 2008 William was presented with his 'wings' by his father: 37 years after Charles had been presented with his 'wings' by the Duke of Edinburgh in September 1971.

In a speech to the graduates, Air Chief Marshal Sir Glenn Torpy, Chief of the Air Staff, said, "This is probably one of the most significant milestones in an aviator's career. It's something that not many people can do and you should be very proud of what you have done."

William's future role should have, in theory, made a career in the military out of the question. He had originally joined the military on a short-service commission lasting three years. But, as Prince Charles had said himself nearly forty years earlier when describing his feelings after practising aerobatics at 25,000 feet, "I can't tell you how rewarding it is when one begins to feel increasingly more professional at some skill." Prince William had proved to himself and others that he could compete with the very best in an environment that makes no allowances for birth or status. Group Captain Nigel Wharmby, the station's commanding officer, made it clear that the graduating students, "…are very special people and that is why we recognise their accomplishments in this ceremony." Military flying is a supreme challenge: William had discovered within himself – as had his father and grandfather before him – an ability to master both the technical skills and possess the quality of intellect (Charles had found navigation skills a struggle to master) needed to meet the challenge.

The announcement when it came was a surprise to everyone. The Prince would be extending his time in the forces, first by taking on another secondment in the autumn of 2008 that would include working at the Ministry of Defence and non-operational flying with the Army Air Corps. He would then transfer from the Army to the Royal Air Force to train as a full time search and rescue helicopter pilot flying Sea King helicopters.

The RAF has its own Search and Rescue Force (SARF) made up of six search and rescue teams in the UK who work alongside four civilian coastguard and two Royal Navy teams. No area in the UK is more than one hour's flight away in daylight and with over a thousand callouts a year, often in adverse weather conditions and over difficult terrain, the crews of search and rescue missions have to be self-sufficient, quick-thinking and resourceful; flying skills can be tested to the utmost. Lives are routinely at stake and, consequently, only the best are selected to fly and crew the missions. Happily for the Prince, on the 16th September 2010 he graduated, along with six other students, from his Search and Rescue training course at Royal Air Force Valley in Anglesey. Shortly thereafter

20 April, 2008: Defence Medical Services Rehabilitation Centre at Headley Court. Prince Harry had trained with 24-year-old Marine Mark Ormrod who lost an arm and both his legs when he stepped on a mine during a routine foot patrol. Marine Ormrod said that Harry's experience on the field of battle made a big difference when he was meeting fellow service people. "He's been out there and he's seen and done it. They are both quite involved and they don't just sit on the sidelines. It makes a difference to us rather than having someone who hasn't experienced it, it makes them more genuine."

he joined C Flight of Number 22 Squadron, based at RAF Valley as a fully qualified and fully operational Search and Rescue pilot. Beginning his operational service as co-pilot of a Sea King Mk3 helicopter and working as part of a four-person crew, William can expect to serve as a Search and Rescue pilot for 36 months. Known as Flight Lieutenant Wales in the RAF, his graduation is the culmination of seven months of training during which he completed 70 hours of live flying plus 50 hours of simulator training, learning how to manoeuvre the Sea King helicopter to the extraordinary high standards expected of Search and Rescue helicopter pilots. "I am really delighted to have completed the training course with my fellow students. The course has been challenging, but I have enjoyed it immensely. I absolutely love flying, so it

will be an honour to serve operationally with the Search and Rescue Force, helping to provide such a vital emergency service."

The logic is compelling: two brothers who have shown both the aptitude and talent for a life in military service, yet who are denied, by the circumstances of their birth and the wider political and security issues of the day, the chance to fulfil their heartfelt aspirations. How must it feel to be always restricted from putting their training to the ultimate test? If by learning to fly operationally they can overcome the obstacles that circumscribe their evident wish to serve with their fellow countryman in theatres of war and disaster – as their great grandfather did in 1916 – then who are we to argue that 'Save ceremony, save general ceremony' is not enough?

18 June, 2009: Flyboys. Princes William and Harry at RAF Shawbury where William trained to become a fully operational RAF Search and Rescue pilot and Harry is training to become a fully operational Army Air Corps pilot.

19 October, 2007: Real Boys Own stuff as Prince William, wearing a black special forces dry-suit, takes part in an exercise simulating an amphibious assault outside the Faslane Naval base on the Clyde.

12 December, 2005: A two-week placement at RAF Valley includes training with a mountain rescue team at Trearddur Bay in North Wales. In due course the Prince will make the decision to become a full-time pilot and join the Royal Air Force's Search and Rescue Force (SARF).

Sqn Ldr J Christen

Mrs N Marsh

Sqn Ldr K Marsh

Miss K Middleton

Fg Off W Wales

Mrs J Allison

Sqn Ldr R Allison

Ms L Johnson

...R Lees

11 April, 2008: It was a horrible, cold and wet day and although the wings ceremony was an important photo-call, it had not promised to be anything out of the ordinary. Suddenly an excited chatter went around the media room when we realised Kate would be Prince William's guest. This would be her first appearance with the Prince at an official ceremony since the Sovereign's Parade at Sandhurst. [RN]

24 April, 2009: During a poignant visit to the National Memorial Arboretum near Lichfield, William sees the name of his Sandhurst platoon commander Major Alexis Roberts of the 1st Battalion The Royal Gurkha Rifles, killed in Afghanistan and Intelligence Officer Joanna Dyer who trained in his platoon and was killed near Basra.

"That girl in the omnibus had one of those faces of marvellous beauty which are seen casually in the streets but never among one's friends. Where do these women come from? Who marries them? Who knows them?"

Thomas Hardy, 1840–1928

CATHERINE

CATHERINE

For a young woman who is the focus of so much media attention, remarkably little is known about the real Kate. Catherine as she is known to her family and friends – it was the media who decided on the shortened form – has never offered a single public utterance, nor has anyone connected with her broken ranks to offer much in the way of an insight beyond a handful of laudatory remarks about her school years.

What little is known amounts to the often repeated facts that she was born at the Royal Berkshire Hospital in Reading on 9 January 1982 to parents Michael Francis Middleton, an airline pilot at the time of her birth, and Carole Elizabeth Middleton (nee Goldsmith) who was a flight attendant. Her father hails from Leeds and Kate's mother's roots hark back to County Durham. Today they own a successful mail order business called Party Pieces. Kate has a younger sister Philippa (known as Pippa) and a younger brother James.

Kate attended St Andrew's School, Pangbourne, until she was thirteen and then went on to Marlborough College, where she was an excellent student. Accepted by Scotland's oldest university, St Andrew's, she would meet fellow History of Art student William Wales in 2001 – and quietly step into the quixotic rarified world of palaces and ceremony, polo and shooting parties and, conceivably, one day be admitted to and live her life at the very heart of this nation's royal family.

For Prince William it is all written in the stars of course, his destiny unalterable. One day he will, "by the Grace of God be King, Head of the Commonwealth, Defender of the Faith of the United Kingdom of Great Britain and Northern Ireland of His other Realms and Territories." Or put more simply, His Majesty King William V – assuming he retains William as his regnal name. If she marries him, level-headed, firmly middle-class, English beauty Kate will become Queen Catherine. Without being unduly morbid – we are talking about the succession of

the monarchy after all – and allowing for the long-lived Windsor genes, the arithmatic is relatively straightforward: Prince William can expect to be crowned king in the next twenty years or so, by which time both he and Kate will be in their late-forties, still in the prime of their lives.

Prince William has seen first-hand how his father has laboured to turn the role of heir apparent into a full-time meaningful job. While waiting for the 'top job' and circumscribed by the constraints of a constitutional monarchy, the Prince has navigated a treacherous path of focussed, passionate social concern and practical community endeavour, perhaps best typified by the Prince's Trust. Begun in 1976, it has stayed true to its original purpose of realising the talent which, Prince Charles argued, lay within even the most recalcitrant of individuals. His time in the Navy had taught him that natural intelligence, raw talent and ability were to be found among young ratings regardless of background.

No-one seriously expects the Queen to abdicate, and when Prince Charles does eventually succeed – possibly well into his seventies – he will clearly wish to rule in his own inimitable fashion. It's the job he has been waiting for all of his life and the clamour for the monarchy to 'skip a generation' during the immediate aftermath of Diana, Princess of Wales's death was as nonsensical as it was hysterical. Charles will be king and William will be invested as the 22nd Prince of Wales. Memories of Diana will have faded to the point where Catherine, Princess of Wales, can assume her rightful place in the hearts of the people without fear of taint or accusations of being a usurper.

Repeatedly Palace officials have said that Prince William understands at the most fundamental level, and accepts fully, the heritage into which he has been born, but, given the sort of timescale outlined above and presumably having no wish to intrude unnecessarily on his father's role, he can see no advantage in rushing into a life of ceremonial and royal and duty. Not when his father upon turning sixty has much work still to do; not when he can take on a meaningful, visible and enjoyable role in the RAF.

So in the latter part of 2010 Flying Officer Wales starts a three year attachment as a fully operational SARF pilot, flying Sea King helicopters initially out of RAF Valley in North Wales. An interesting moment as he takes on a full time military role having successfully completed his training. "I don't want to get married until 28 or 30", he once said, and in 2010, just as he undertakes his first attachment, the Prince will be 28.

Predicting the immediate future for Kate is more of a challenge. With a brief interruption from April to June 2007 – and even this so-called split might have had rather less to it than met the eye – William and Kate have had a relationship for a number of years. She has attended most of the significant and public milestones in the Prince's life including their joint graduation ceremony at St Andrews, the Sovereign's Parade at Sandhurst, the wings ceremony at RAF Cranwell and his installation as a Knight of the Most Noble Order of the Garter at Windsor. She has joined him at the annual skiing sojourn in the Alps and been on holiday with him several times. Kate is clearly at ease in the company of Prince William's friends, and with his father as the pictures taken of the Royal Box at Cheltenham Festival and on the ski slopes bear testament. And by all accounts the Queen has offered her a warm welcome into the family. By British society's usual standards it would be safe to describe Kate as William's 'serious' girlfriend.

The trouble with this analysis is that the notion of a long-term 'girlfriend' is pretty much without royal precedent. Diana went, it seemed, from the 'jolly and bouncy' unaffected teenager who Prince Charles had met when at her ancestral home, Althorpe – where he had been invited by his then girlfriend and Diana's older sister Sarah – to his fiancée with nothing much in between, and it must be said with no great evidence of a surge in his feelings.

Diana's background meant that she would, in theory at least, have had enough knowledge of the workings of the royal family to have few fears of marrying into it. Kate, on the other hand, must surely be seen by many courtiers as an altogether more long-term and time-consuming project. She has to be moulded to the special needs of the institution and while she retains the ambiguous royal status of girlfriend, the process, one imagines, can only be managed by way of an informal and *ad hoc* regime.

And here is a cautionary note: World War I did a splendid job of demolishing the time-honoured practice of European monarchies marrying among themselves. After the war there were no longer enough royal brides and bridegrooms to go around.

George V gave permission for his younger son, Albert, Duke of York, to marry Lady Elizabeth Bowes-Lyon who was legally a commoner though the daughter of a peer. At the time the engagement was considered a gesture in favour of political modernisation and thereafter the certainty that royal would marry royal was pretty much consigned to history. The legacy has, when viewed objectively, been disastrous. With the exceptions of the marriages of the Queen Mother, every significant example of British royalty marrying a commoner has ended in divorce: Princess Anne and Captain Mark Phillips, the Duke and Duchess of York and the Prince and Princess of Wales. Whether this is a state of affairs that merely reflects a wider society issue or is a deep-seated problem caused by the way the royal family relates to outsiders is open to debate.

The royal family, by inclination and training, live in a world of contained feelings and regimented activity. They expect those who marry into the family to assume their rigid code and behaviour, but they also learn from their mistakes and to a certain extent move with the times. If Kate has been given any sort of unofficial but internally significant status, then it must be something the Queen herself has decided upon – so that Kate is included more, gets to know the way things work and the people involved.

The Queen has a widely acknowledged strong work ethic – arguably, it has been her unswerving commitment to duty that has kept the monarchy safe from the combined ravages of scandal and nascent republicanism over the last fifteen years – and while reports of Kate's school years and the degree she earned at St Andrew's indicate that Kate is anything but work shy, there is something at odds with the monarchy's determination to appear modern and forward looking to have the girlfriend of the future heir to the throne perceived (quite wrongly) as not doing very much apart from waiting.

The trouble is, if a marriage between William and Kate is being seriously contemplated, then, however unfashionable it might be, for now, Kate's career options are limited. She is already in a life she can't dictate and in a role as girlfriend to the future heir to the throne that makes perpetual but intermittent demands on her requires constant flexibility and commitment.

Moving back in with your mother and father at the age of twenty-seven may seem a retrograde step for many university educated young women, but for a woman in a serious relationship with the second in line to the throne, it is easy to see why it might be considered the safest and most sensible solution. In any case, even in modern Britain, being wife to the future king will require her to give up any career she might have chosen.

10 May, 2009: Polo at Coworth Park, Ascot. "Love seems the swiftest, but it is the slowest of all growths. No man or woman really knows what perfect love is until they have been married a quarter of a century." Mark Twain.

1 June, 1983: The Princess of Wales and the Duchess of York at Polo. Diana's jumper launched a thousand imitations.

29 July, 2006: Smith's Lawn, Windsor – the grounds of The Guards Polo Club.

7 June, 2009: Cirencester Park Polo Club. Endless public curiosity and the vigilant presence of the media will make Kate the most scrutinized woman on the planet. Already extraordinary steps are being taken to offer her snatched moments of privacy, even at the most public of events.

19 June, 1996: Diana had travelled to Rome as a guest of the fashion designer Krizia whose show she would be attending that evening. Diana and her escort left Rome airport at high speed while we, the accompanying media, headed straight for our hotel that happened to be situated at the top of the Spanish Steps. I'd just checked in when I heard an unusual noise that soon escalated to a roar. It was coming from the foot of the Steps and within minutes a crowd of what must have been two thousand or more had gathered. Without even seeing Diana, I instinctively knew she must be the sole reason for the commotion. It became clear that Diana was trying to have a coffee in the famous Antico Caffè Greco. I couldn't get anywhere near so I took this photograph from the top of the Steps. It shows what an extraordinary magnetism Diana had and, no matter where she was in the world, she would always attract a huge following. Will Kate have to live with such global attention? [RN]

4 May, 2007: Badminton Horse Trials which take place each year in the grounds of Badminton House, Gloucestershire.

28 May, 1983: Diana waits and watches while Prince Charles plays polo at Windsor.

22 June, 2008: Beaufort Polo Club and Kate waits while Prince William plays polo for the Tusk Trust.

(Previous page) **1 August, 2007:** Early morning on the Thames at Chiswick, London.

16 March, 2007: Gold Cup Day
at the Cheltenham National
Hunt Festival.

"The novelties of one generation
are only the resuscitated fashions
of the generation before last."
George Bernard Shaw 1856–1950

6

A LIFE LESS
ORDINARY

A LIFE LESS ORDINARY

A sun-kissed afternoon in London almost a decade since thousands had last gathered with Diana, Princess of Wales, in mind, but this time the mood was one of joyous celebration, rather than over-powering grief.

Timed to mark what would have been Diana's 46th birthday, the concert, organised by Princes William and Harry, reflected their mother's special talent of appealing to just about everybody, and would feature a roster of stars from the worlds of pop, hip hop, rock, stage musicals and ballet. 65,000 would pack into Wembley Stadium, although noticeable absentees would include the senior members of the royal family – this was the Princes' tribute, and the concert would be broadcast live in 140 different countries, watched by an audience of hundreds of millions. At the end of a long day and many great performances, a moving video montage of Diana as a child – accompanied by the Queen song *These Are the Days of Our Lives* – flickered into life on giant screens on the stage. As the final echoes of the song faded and the last poignant image of a pretty young girl on the lawns of Althorp faded, many in the stadium and around the world would have been reminded that for a while at least, Diana had been the greatest star of all.

Two months later on 31 August 2007, exactly ten years from the day Diana died, family and friends joined the Princes William and Harry for a thanksgiving service for the life of Diana at the Guards' Chapel near Buckingham Palace. Prince Harry, who was 12 when his mother was killed, told the congregation, which included the Queen, Prince Philip and Prince Charles, "She made us and so many other people happy." He went on to say that her death was, "Indescribably shocking and sad", and had changed his life and that of his brother forever.

Before the service there had been considerable debate about whether the Bishop of London, the Right Reverend Dr Richard Chartres, should conduct the service. A friend of Prince Charles since their days together at Cambridge University in the 1970s, it was claimed by many close to the Princess that he had hardly known Diana, meeting her on just a handful of occasions. Nevertheless, during his address Dr Chartres offered a convincing and undoubtedly sincere eulogy that managed to encapsulate Diana's unique empathetic qualities and locate the use to which she put her remarkable talent at the very heart of a modern-day constitutional monarchy. "There is a properly political sphere in which the monarch may counsel but doesn't intrude, but there is another sphere, vital to any sense of national unity and creativity, a sphere in which communities must be celebrated, common values articulated and the transcendent source of those values honoured. And at a time when people are suspicious of rhetoric, the monarchy communicates by symbol and by simple speech, and the Princess brought her own gifts to this work."

In typifying how Diana used her position – scarcely diminished by her divorce from Charles and arguably the royal family itself – and extraordinary ability to relate to all those she came into contact with (her close friend Rosa Monckton called it "intuitive genius"), Dr Chartres also reaffirmed the immense good Diana was capable of doing; he brought into focus the permanent need for the monarchy to affirm all that is best in its people and bring about a sense of unity and nationhood. "She was still only 26 in 1987 when she shook the hand of a patient at the opening of the Middlesex Hospital's AIDS ward. It was the first in the UK and it is very hard now to credit the degree of fear and prejudice which surrounded AIDS in the 80s. Those familiar with the field have no doubt that the Princess played a significant part in overcoming a harmful and even a cruel taboo in a gesture which was not choreographed but sprung from a deep identification with those who were vulnerable and on the margin."

In the last few weeks of her life, with the active encouragement of Great Britain's new Prime Minister, Tony Blair, Diana found a renewed energy and had committed herself to the campaign aiming to rid the world of the scourge of landmines. A trip to war-torn Angola in association with the British Red Cross had, on the one hand, raised political hackles – a Conservative junior minister of the government of the day describing her as a 'loose cannon' – and, more importantly, public awareness of this massively-deserving cause.

The newly elected British Labour government responded to the consequent swell of public outrage by banning the export and use of landmines, and pressure was brought to bear on the Clinton administration to undertake a similar policy re-think.

The Princess, keen to visit other affected countries, decided on a trip to Bosnia, still recovering from civil war. She would travel with the distinguished journalist Lord Deedes. Describing her ability to communicate across cultural barriers he remarked, "She was one who sought above all to help vulnerable people in society and who did it so well. She was good at this because she herself was vulnerable. She knew the feeling. She didn't set out to be a saint."

Three weeks later in the early hours of 31 August 1997 a black Mercedes 220SL entered the Place de l'Alma underpass on the north bank of the Seine and seconds later the brightest star in the British royal firmament was cruelly extinguished.

Let Fame, that all hunt after in their lives,
Live registered upon our brazen tomb,
And then grace us in the disgrace of death;

Words spoken by the King of Navarre in Shakespeare's play *Love's Labour's Lost* – a king who seeks to avoid death's worse consequences – descent into inevitable anonymity as time marches ever on. Diana had once claimed that she wanted to avoid being celebrated for 'being', but to be valued for 'doing' – in words and deeds. So much of the role of the monarchy is just being, yet traditionally fame has always been the consequence of 'doing'. Actors, footballers, musicians, writers and successful politicians do what they do extremely well for the most part, earning our respect and from this respect 'old-style' fame emerges. And with fame comes scrutiny, the weight of expectation and sometimes great power.

The royal family is unique in being dissociated from the underlying mechanism of fame – its members are, quite literally, born into it. Fame – sometimes of a dubious sort – is certainly thrust upon them. While serving as symbols of continuity and the state, carrying out largely ceremonial functions, the monarch's traditional point is to be someone we hardly ever approach in real life, but lives in our heads in a place where we formulate our common sense of the nation-state and social identity. It's a perilous business: while continuing to reject the European trend towards socially-levelled bicycling monarchs, we expect our royal family to be bejewelled and glamorous, talismanic and the main players in a themed pageant. Or, alternatively, figures that are all too human with evident feet of clay whose betrayals and failings can be paraded across the pages of newspapers.

We live in a society that is culturally and intellectually the product of the Age of Enlightenment, a liberal democratic society that prides individualism and choice – the freedom to act and to become all you can be. The flipside of individualism is a condition we have arguably slipped into: an increasingly ghastly quagmire of relativism that plaintively insists that all choices are equal – underage unmarried motherhood as an acceptable life choice springs to mind – and that a facile form of fame without 'doing' is a birthright of all. The nineteenth-century journalist and editor of *The Economist*, Walter Bagehot, in describing the special purpose and place of the monarchy in the hearts and minds of its subjects, wrote that, "We must not let daylight in upon the magic."

It's probably a bit late for that now: the twentieth-century equivalent of daylight, Cyclopean television cameras, have been mercilessly unmasking the *léger de main* of the Crown ever since Prince Edward foisted the supremely embarrassing *It's A Royal Knockout* (1987) on an unsuspecting and unprepared public; Prince Charles' dialogue with his amanuensis Jonathan Dimbleby on the lawns at Highgrove (1994), and Diana stunned the nation with her emotional *cri de coeur* on *Panorama* (1995). The slow erosion of respect for the monarchy suggests that the time is approaching when the curtain will come down on the greatest conjuring trick of the last thousand years.

Somehow it all comes back to Diana. She was utterly modern, clearly beloved and, somehow, entirely apart from the rest of us. The sort of royal we would elect if we had that choice. Semi-divorced from the royal family she may have been, but in the people's hearts she was still very much 'our' princess.

The world hankers for a new Diana-like figure, which makes Kate Middleton's appearance at the Concert for Diana all the more significant. Two and a half months earlier the *Sun* newspaper headline had announced their 'split'. Yet here she was sitting in the Royal Box albeit at some distance from the Prince. A few weeks later it was clear that the relationship was back on.

To the future: Prince Charles when he succeeds to the throne may be the last act. He will reign with one foot firmly anchored in the traditions and duties of the job for which he has trained all his life, and the other in a forward looking concerned intellectualism, pointedly directed at the politicians, agro-industrialists and urban planners of the day.

Meanwhile, the problem for Kate as she spirals into the very heart of the sun is that she maybe errs too much on the side of beauty. If she becomes Princess Catherine then the picture on page 96 of *Diana in Rome* is a powerful portent. Every camera lens in the world will hunger for her. The question is will she find the right sort of modern-day fame visited upon her? Will she be celebrated for 'being' – a beautifully dressed, ever-smiling adornment to the House of Windsor – or, by 'doing' in both words and deeds, reach for the star quality and healing spirit of Diana. We have so little to presently go on that only time will tell. Let King of Navarre have the last words:

When, spite of cormorant devouring Time,
Th'endeavour of this present breath may buy
That honour which shall bate his scythe's keen edge,
And make us heirs of all eternity.

16 June, 2010: For the first time the Princes carry out joint engagements overseas. They travel to Africa where they visit a traditional Lesotho herdboy nightschool on a freezing cold night in the remote mountain village of Semongkong.

17 June, 2010: The Princes ride into town on a visit to Semengkong Children's centre.

19 June, 2010: Princes William and Harry meet David Beckham during the FIFA World Cup in South Africa.

15 January, 2010: William and Kate share a moment at the ceremony held at RAF Shawbury where the Prince moved one step closer to becoming a search and rescue pilot having completed an advanced helicopter training course. Kate was later seen to applaud enthusiastically as Prince Charles awarded William his 'new' Wings.

24 April, 2009: Another pressing engagement. However much William enjoys meeting his subjects to be, a royal walkabout is a strictly timetabled affair. The Prince's Private Secretary keeps an eagle eye on his watch.

24 April, 2009: Something very British. One day he will be Head of State of the United Kingdom and 15 other Commonwealth realms, but today on a visit to the headquarters of JCB, William is at the heart of a very British welcome.

21 February, 2010: William arrives at London's Royal Opera House for the Orange British Academy Film Awards and proves a great hit with waiting film fans. He succeeds Lord Attenborough as the fifth President of the British Academy of Film and Television Arts following in his grandfather's steps who became BAFTA's first president in 1959. The Presidency marks Prince William's most significant honorary appointment in the arts world to date.

22 February, 2010: A Prince and his people. On his first official visit to Liverpool, William visits Alder Hey Children's Hospital to officially launch a new £3 million life-saving MRI scanner. "I just go and meet people and just enjoy their company. . . I really enjoy it, I get a buzz out of it. Seeing kids smile means a lot to me."

17 January, 2010: At the end of his first day of a three day visit to New Zealand, William watches the lifting of the hangi out of the pit for dinner while the Governor-General, Sir Anand Satyanand, supervises.

18 January, 2010: William is to open the new Supreme Court in Wellington as the Queen's representative; the first time he has represented his grandmother in an official capacity. He arrives to a traditional Maori greeting and is presented with the gift of a korowai (feather cloak) from Te Papa (the National Museum of New Zealand).

Overleaf:
18 January, 2010: William chews that fat with New Zealand's Prime Minister John Key and helps to get the barbecue going at Premier House in Wellington.

18 January, 2010: Despite the presence of a low-key republican demonstration nearby, over one thousand fans turned up to enthusiastically greet William outside the Supreme Court. One young girl, Melissa Moroney, said, as the Maori cloak was draped on William's shoulders that it was, "A once in a life time opportunity to see him in the flesh. You can't really pass that up".

21 January, 2010: It's not entirely certain she knows who he is. William cooks at a community barbeque in Flowerdale, a bushfire-devastated town 100km north of Melbourne.

19 January, 2010: As patron of Centrepoint, the charity for young homeless in London, William visits a shelter for the homeless in Sydney with Australian Prime Minister Kevin Rudd.

19 January, 2010: The local reaction to William's visit to Australia demonstrates that republicanism still faces hefty opposition. All sorts of well-wishers and fans wanted to see the Prince in the flesh. Up close and personable.

16 June, 2008: The Queen appoints His Royal Highness
Prince William of Wales to be a Royal Knight Companion of
the Most Noble Order of the Garter half a century after his
father received the same honour.

27 June, 2008: At her most beautiful. Kate attends the 46664 concert in celebration of Nelson Mandela's life.

19 July, 2008: Kate attends the wedding of Lady Rose Windsor, the 28-year-old daughter of the Duke of Gloucester, the Queen's cousin. A clear indication of her growing intimacy with the royal family.

"Give a girl an education and
introduce her properly into the
world, and ten to one but she
has the means of settling well,
without further expense to
anybody."

Jane Austen, 1775–1887

7

FOR BETTER
OR WORSE

FOR BETTER OR WORSE

"Once upon a time there was a young man. He was, perhaps, not a frog at the beginning of the fairytale first told by the Grimm brothers, but he was certainly not a prince. The first kiss did not change that. His transformation was not possible without the support of the wise king and queen who had ruled the kingdom for many years and who were full of wisdom and had good hearts. They knew what was best and guided the young couple with a gentle hand generously sharing all their valuable experience."

Prince Daniel, Duke of Västergötland from his speech on the occasion of his marriage to Crown Princess Victoria of Sweden.

'I think people really marry far too much; it is such a lottery after all,' wrote Queen Victoria in a letter to her daughter in 1858. Victoria had won, arguably, that particular lottery, enjoying a loving and happy marriage to Prince Albert of Saxe-Coburg and Gotha to whom she had proposed in 1839. Married in the Chapel Royal of St. James's Palace, Albert, Prince Consort would prove not only Victoria's irreplaceable companion, but an important advisor replacing the young Queen's mentor Viscount Melbourne as the most influential figure in the first half of her reign.

In 1861, during a deeply troublesome year, Albert was diagnosed with typhoid fever and on the 14th December died in the Blue Room at Windsor Castle. Victoria, still deeply affected by the death of her mother earlier in the year, was, by all accounts, utterly devastated. Their 21-year marriage had produced nine children and 42 grandchildren who married into royal families across the European continent earning Victoria the nickname 'the grandmother of Europe.'

13 years after the death of Queen Victoria, the horrors of the First World War and its immediate Spanish influenza pandemic aftermath put paid to the enduring practice of royals marrying royals. Without enough eligible scions of the royal houses of Europe to go around, marriage to commoners, albeit of noble birth more or less, would be the new order of things. And so it has remained. As the

19 June, 2010: Crown Princess Mette-Marit of Norway at the wedding of Crown Princess Victoria of Sweden.

House of Windsor contemplates the possible marriage of the second in the line of succession to a young woman of impeccable middle class forbears, it is interesting to examine a number of modern-day royal marriages across Europe and ask what lessons can be learnt.

In 1980 Sweden revised its constitution to adopt royal succession by absolute (or equal) primogeniture. This had the effect of displacing the reigning monarch King Carl XVI Gustaf and his wife Queen Silvia's infant son Carl Philip in favour of their eldest daughter Crown Princess Victoria Ingrid Alice Désirée – who would eventually be Queen. In 2002 the 24-year-old, one of the most eligible princesses in Europe, hired a new personal trainer – a young sports-mad Daniel Westling. As the Victoria would explain during the couple's engagement interview, she had first met Daniel at his gym. They had become friends at first and had not, as the fairytales would have us believe, fallen in love at first sight, nor, according to Daniel, had the first kiss turned the frog into a prince. Love, however, did indeed creep up on the couple and their engagement was announced at the Royal Palace in Stockholm on 24 February 2009. "With Daniel by my side I feel secure," she said. "You have probably noticed that in recent years I have seemed stronger and happier. And now the time has come for us to begin building something together and starting a family."

In a beautiful ceremony held at Stockholm Cathedral on 19th June 2010, the couple were married to massive popular acclaim. It was the first Swedish royal wedding since the marriage of King Gustaf to Queen Silvia in 1976, and the first wedding of a female heir to the throne in the history of Sweden.

Sweden had eight years to grow accustomed to the prospect of their beloved Princess marrying a rather ordinary gym-owning commoner. Inevitably, some voices have been heard criticising his lack of aristocratic heritage, asking whether he is a suitable partner for the future Queen of Sweden. His mother-in-law has spoken out vigorously in his defence, "I think he's going to do well," said Queen Silvia, who is also not of royal descent, in a TV interview. "He's going to be successful in his task of helping the Princess."

In a country not so very far away, a rather different story of royal romance was unfolding. In fact it was such an unlikely engagement that it caused the then president of Norway's parliament, Kirsti Kolle Grøndahl, to suggest to the country's four million citizens that concening the early life of Mette-Marit Tjessem Høiby: "I think it's wise for all of us to put this in the past and not let it tarnish her future."

Mette-Marit was born on August 19, 1973, the youngest child of Marit Tjessem, a bank officer, and Sven Olav Bjarte

Høiby, a journalist. In July 1996 she met the future King of Norway, His Royal Highness Crown Prince Hakkon at the Quart Festival in Kristiansand, Mette-Marit's hometown. Pregnant at the time with her first son Marius, it would be three years before she met the Prince again at the same venue. Love seems to have struck quickly and without complication. In May 2000 Crown Prince Haakon gave an interview to NRK (the Norwegian state owned broadcaster) telling the Norwegian people that yes, he had a girlfriend and she had a child. Beforehand there had been a lot of speculation in the Norwegian media about the relationship. In the following September the Crown Prince bought a flat in Oslo where the three (she with her son Marius) moved in together. Their engagement was announced soon after.

Virgil may have written that love conquers all, but love was going to have its work cut out on this occasion. Suddenly Mette-Marit's life was a matter of national scrutiny: she had a three-year-old son, Marius, by another man and, inevitably, many questioned the Crown Prince's choice of partner. Slowly but surely Mette-Marit was seen to be adapting gracefully to her new life. The royal family evidently offered its support and her courageous statement, made during a pre-wedding press conference where a clearly distressed Mette-Marit holding on to Prince Hakkon's hand confessed to the nation that she regretted her wild past, won her praise and the increased support of the population. Today happily married to the Prince and as the proud mother of three children, the Crown Princess is a hugely popular figure – love did conquer after all.

A horse-mad young Australian girl with hopes to become a veterinarian can hardly have imagined what life would have in store for her; her story is truly a modern-day fairytale romance. Mary Elizabeth Donaldson, the youngest of four children of Scottish-born mathematician Professor John Dalgleish Donaldson and Henrietta "Etta" Clark Donaldson, was raised in Tasmania. After graduating Mary would go on to have a successful business career. Her life would change forever when, in the year 2000 during the Sydney Olympic Games, she met in a pub, quite by chance, the future King of Denmark, His Royal Highness Crown Prince Frederik of Denmark, who simply introduced himself as Fred. The attraction was immediate, as Prince Frederik would make clear during his somewhat metaphysical wedding speech four years later. A long distance relationship followed until at the end of 2001 Mary moved to Europe. Often seen in Denmark with Frederik, it was widely assumed she was the Crown Prince's girlfriend. The Queen however had made a demanding set of requirements before she would agree to their marriage: Mary would have

to relinquish her Australian citizenship; convert from her Presbyterian faith to the Danish Lutheran Church and learn Danish. On 24 September 2003 the Danish court announced that Queen Margrethe II intended to give her consent to the marriage at the State Council meeting on 8 October 2003 and the couple became officially engaged the same day. "Today is the first day of my new role," Mary said after appearing on the palace balcony as Frederik's fiancée for the first time. "It is something that will evolve over time and I have much to learn and experience." Now the mother of two children and with twins expected in early 2011, Her Royal Highness Crown Princess Mary of Denmark with her beauty, grace and popular touch has completely won over the people of her new homeland. Proving that distance and language need not be barriers to a fairytale happy ending.

Three consorts who have overcome the tyranny of distance, language and background to win the love of their spouses, the acceptance of immediate royal families and the respect and admiration of their future subjects.

In fact the same pattern of fairytale meetings, difficulties surmounted, resistance worn down and stable loving family lives built under the relentless glare of public scrutiny, that is the lot of every heir to a throne, can be witnessed across Europe.

In Monaco Charlene Wittstock, born in the former British colony of Rhodesia, now Zimbabwe, is set to marry Prince Albert in July 2011. The Prince and Charlene met first in 2000 at a swimming competition and have been seen together since 2006. Charlene is a former South African Olympic swimming team member and has had to learn French and the Monégasque dialect to marry her prince.

Controversy arose in 2001 when it became clear that Willem-Alexander, Prince of Orange, heir to the Kingdom of the Netherlands, was contemplating marriage to Argentinean born investment banker Máxima Zorreguieta. Her politician father, Jorge Horacio Zorreguieta Stefanini, had served under the regime of General Jorge Rafael Videla, a military dictator responsible for many atrocities against the Argentinean people. His presence at the wedding would have been a serious embarrassment to the Dutch royal household, but in the end her father elected not to attend the wedding. The couple were married on 2 February 2002 and are now the proud parents of three children. Crown Princess Máxima has long since won the affection of the

19 June, 2010: The wedding of Crown Princess Victoria of Sweden to Daniel Westling in Stockholm. In a speech Victoria thanked the people of Sweden for giving her her new prince. During the day Prince Daniel movingly compared himself to the Grimm's fairy tale frog turned into a prince by the kiss of his beautiful bride.

Dutch people with her warmth, spontaneity and obvious intelligence along with her commitment to her royal role and as a constant supporter of Willem-Alexander.

Tall, dark and undoubtedly handsome, Prince Felipe of Spain has, in the past, been linked with a number of beautiful women; he was, for many years, arguably one of the most eligible men in Europe. He had said on more than one occasion that whomsoever he chose to marry, it would be "a relationship based on love, respect and kindness". True to his word, the surprise announcement in 2003 of his engagement to 31-year-old newsreader Letizia Ortiz Rocasolano – a commoner, divorcée and much liked public figure was, in fact, warmly welcomed by the country: "a Queen for the 21st century" was the popular headline.

Returning for a moment to the mid-nineteenth century, it had been Leopold I, first King of the Belgians, who from 1837 sort to arrange the marriage of his niece Queen Victoria to his nephew, and Victoria's cousin, Prince Albert. Today, Prince Philippe, Duke of Brabant, Prince of Belgium is the eldest son and heir apparent of Albert II, King of the Belgians and Queen Paola. Seemingly a confirmed bachelor in his late thirties, there were suggestions that he step aside in favour of his younger sister Princess Astrid, but rather late in the day the announcement of his engagement to Mathilde d'Udekem d'Acoz, a 23-year old speech therapist came as a complete surprise to many.

Princess Malthide is the daughter of the Count and Countess Patrick d'Udekem d'Acoz, so while not exactly of royal birth, she is drawn from the aristocracy and although Brussels-born and of Flemish ancestry was raised at her family seat in the French speaking Wallonia – thus bridging the difficult ethnic and language divisions that are associated with the country.

So in Europe today we see examples of royal marriages forged out of love, common purpose and optimism. Resistance and difficulties have been overcome, hard work, glamour and steadfastness have secured the affection of their nation's people and international respect. There is much for a young royal couple anticipating marriage to live up to here, and much for us all to look forward to.

'What greater thing is there for two human souls than to feel that they are joined for life – to strengthen each other in all labour, to rest on each other in all sorrow, to minister to each other in all pain, to be one with each other in silent unspeakable memories at the moment of the last parting?'

George Eliot, Adam Bede

8 September, 2004: A Princess greatly loved by the Swedish people, Victoria attends a gala dinner in Reykjavik.

Clockwise from the top left: 19 June, 2010: Her Royal Highness Doña Letizia, Princess of Asturias; Princess Mathilde, Duchess of Brabant; Her Royal Highness Crown Princess Mary of Denmark and Her Royal Highness Máxima, Princess of the Netherlands all photographed at the wedding of Crown Princess Victoria of Sweden.

THE ENGAGEMENT OF
PRINCE WILLIAM AND KATE MIDDLETON

16 NOVEMBER 2010

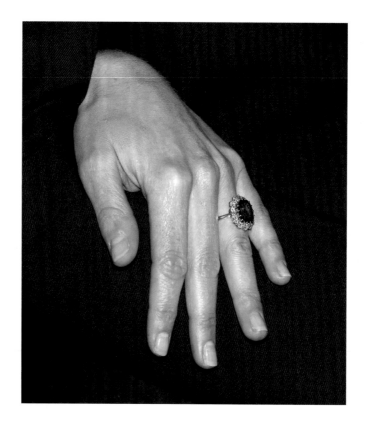

My sincere thanks to

Aasta – the most knowledgeable
royal photo archivist in the business.

Jonathan – who takes the raw
ingredients and makes them work.
Photographers – Aasta, Jim, Kelvin & Michael

Contributors to, and organisers of, the royal rota.
The best organised royal photographic pool system anywhere.

Robin Nunn